Keanu Reeves

The Life and Career of Keanu Reeves

Universal Publishing World

All rights reserved. No part of this publication may be reproduced, distributed, or transmitted in any form or by any means, including photocopying, recording, or other electronic or mechanical methods without the publisher's prior written permission, except in the case of brief quotation embodied in critical reviews permitted by copyright law.

Copyright ©Universal Publishing World 2023.

Keanu Reeves

Table of Content

Introduction

Chapter 1: Early Life and Background

Chapter 2: Career Beginnings

Chapter 3: Breakthrough Roles

Chapter 4: The Matrix Trilogy

Chapter 5: Action Star Status

Chapter 6: Philanthropy and Personal Life

Chapter 7: Career Resurgence

Chapter 8: John Wick Franchise

Keanu Reeves

Chapter 9: Other Notable Films

Chapter 10: Awards and Recognition

Conclusion

Introduction

Keanu Reeves is a Canadian actor, producer, and musician who has captivated audiences with his versatile performances and magnetic screen presence. Born on September 2, 1964, in Beirut, Lebanon, Reeves has become one of Hollywood's most beloved and respected actors. From his early beginnings in the entertainment industry to his iconic roles in films such as "The Matrix" trilogy and the "John Wick" franchise, Reeves has proven himself to be a talented and versatile actor. This table of contents will take a closer look at his life, career, and the impact he has made in the world of cinema.

Reeves' journey in the entertainment industry started at a young age when he began acting in school plays. His passion for performing arts led him to attend the Etobicoke School of the Arts in Toronto, where he honed his craft and developed his acting skills. After graduating, Reeves pursued his acting career and quickly gained recognition for his talent and dedication.

In the early years of his career, Reeves appeared in several television shows and films, gradually building a reputation for his ability to portray a wide range of characters. It was his breakthrough role as Ted Logan in the 1989 film "Bill & Ted's Excellent

Adventure" that catapulted him into the spotlight and made him a household name. The film's success led to a sequel, "Bill & Ted's Bogus Journey," further solidifying Reeves' status as a rising star.

However, it was his portrayal of Neo in the groundbreaking science fiction film "The Matrix" in 1999 that truly cemented Reeves' status as a Hollywood heavyweight. The film, directed by the Wachowski siblings, revolutionized the action genre with its innovative visual effects and thought-provoking storyline. Reeves' performance as the chosen one, fighting against a dystopian reality, showcased his ability to seamlessly blend physicality and emotional depth.

Following the success of "The Matrix," Reeves continued to take on diverse and challenging roles, further showcasing his range as an actor. He starred in films such as "Speed," "The Devil's Advocate," and "Constantine," proving his ability to excel in both action-packed blockbusters and thought-provoking dramas.

Beyond his acting career, Reeves is also known for his philanthropic efforts and humble demeanor. Despite his fame and success, he has remained grounded and down-to-earth, often going out of his way to show kindness and generosity to those around him. He has been involved in various charitable organizations, including Stand Up to Cancer and PETA, using his platform to make a positive impact on the world.

In recent years, Reeves has experienced a career resurgence with the highly successful "John Wick" franchise. The action-packed films have not only showcased his physical prowess but also his ability to bring depth and complexity to his characters. Reeves' commitment to his craft and his dedication to delivering compelling performances have solidified his status as one of Hollywood's most respected and sought-after actors.

Throughout his career, Reeves has received numerous awards and accolades for his work, including a star on the Hollywood Walk of

Keanu Reeves

Fame. His contributions to the film industry have left an indelible mark, and his performances continue to inspire and entertain audiences worldwide.

Chapter 1

Early Life and Background

Keanu Charles Reeves was born on September 2, 1964, in Beirut, Lebanon. His mother, Patricia Taylor, was a costume designer, and his father, Samuel Nowlin Reeves Jr., was a geologist. Reeves' parents met in Beirut while his father was working as a geologist for an American oil company. However, their marriage did not last long, and they divorced when Reeves was just three years old.

After the divorce, Reeves and his mother moved to Australia, where they lived for a short period before relocating to New York City. Eventually, they settled in Toronto, Canada, where Reeves spent most of his childhood. Growing up, Reeves had a multicultural background, with English, Irish, Portuguese, and Native Hawaiian ancestry.

Reeves attended several different schools during his childhood, as his family frequently moved around. He struggled with dyslexia, which made academic life challenging for him. However, he found solace in the performing arts and discovered a passion for acting at a young age.

At the age of nine, Reeves made his acting debut in a school production of "Damn Yankees." This experience ignited his love for the stage and set him on a path towards a career in the entertainment industry. Recognizing his talent and passion, Reeves' mother enrolled him in the Etobicoke School of the Arts in Toronto, a specialized high school for students interested in the arts.

It was at the Etobicoke School of the Arts that Reeves began to develop his acting skills and immerse himself in the world of theater. He performed in various school plays and gained valuable experience that would later shape his career.

Despite his early success in acting, Reeves faced personal tragedy during his teenage years. His close friend, River Phoenix, who was also a rising star in Hollywood, tragically passed away from a drug overdose in 1993. This loss had a profound impact on Reeves and further fueled his determination to succeed in the entertainment industry.

Chapter 2

Career Beginnings

Keanu Reeves' career in the entertainment industry began in the early 1980s when he started appearing in various television shows and small film roles. His first credited role was in the 1984 Canadian drama film "One Step Away," where he played Ron Petrie, a troubled teenager. Although the film didn't receive much attention, it marked the beginning of Reeves' journey as an actor.

Reeves continued to take on small roles in both television and film throughout the 1980s. He appeared in popular Canadian television shows such as "Hangin' In" and "Night Heat," showcasing his talent and versatility as an actor. These early experiences provided Reeves with valuable on-set experience and helped him gain recognition within the industry.

In 1986, Reeves landed a supporting role in the critically acclaimed drama film "River's Edge." His performance as Matt, a troubled teenager dealing with the aftermath of a murder, garnered positive reviews from critics and showcased his ability to portray complex and emotionally charged characters. The film's success further solidified Reeves' reputation as a promising young actor.

Reeves' breakthrough role came in 1989 when he was cast as Ted Logan in the comedy film "Bill & Ted's Excellent Adventure." The film, directed by Stephen Herek, followed the adventures of two high school friends who travel through time in a phone booth. Reeves' portrayal of the lovable and dim-witted Ted showcased his comedic timing and charm, earning him widespread acclaim and a dedicated fan base.

The success of "Bill & Ted's Excellent Adventure" led to a sequel, "Bill & Ted's Bogus Journey," in 1991. Reeves reprised his role as Ted, further solidifying his status as a rising star in Hollywood. The film, although not as commercially successful as its predecessor, showcased Reeves' ability to bring depth and humor to his characters.

While Reeves gained recognition for his comedic roles, he also sought to challenge himself as an actor by taking on more dramatic and diverse roles. In 1991, he starred alongside River Phoenix in the critically acclaimed drama film "My Own Private Idaho." Reeves' portrayal of Scott Favor, a young hustler searching for his identity, showcased his ability to tackle complex and emotionally demanding characters.

Chapter 3

Breakthrough Roles

Keanu Reeves has several breakthrough roles throughout his career. One of his most iconic breakthrough roles was as Neo in the science fiction film "The Matrix" (1999). This role catapulted Reeves to international fame and established him as an action star.

Another breakthrough role for Reeves was his portrayal of John Wick in the "John Wick" film series (2014-present). His performance as the skilled assassin garnered critical acclaim and solidified his status as an action hero.

Reeves also had a breakthrough role in the romantic drama "The Lake House" (2006), where he played opposite Sandra Bullock. This film showcased his versatility as an actor and demonstrated his ability to excel in different genres.

Furthermore, Reeves had a breakthrough role in the science fiction thriller "Speed" (1994), where he played a police officer trying to save a bus from exploding. This film showcased his ability to handle intense action sequences and further cemented his place in Hollywood.

In addition to his action and thriller roles, Keanu Reeves has also had breakthrough performances in other genres. One notable example is his portrayal of Siddhartha Gautama in the historical drama "Little Buddha" (1993). This role allowed Reeves to showcase his dramatic acting skills and explore more philosophical themes.

Another breakthrough role for Reeves was in the romantic comedy "Something's Gotta Give" (2003), where he played a younger love interest to Diane Keaton's character. This film demonstrated his ability to bring charm and humor to his performances, expanding his range as an actor.

Reeves also had a breakthrough role in the science fiction film "The Day the Earth Stood Still" (2008), where he played an alien visitor to Earth. This role showcased his ability to portray complex and otherworldly characters, further establishing him as a versatile actor.

Furthermore, Reeves had a breakthrough role in the martial arts film "Man of Tai Chi" (2013), where he not only starred in the film but also made his directorial debut. This project allowed him to explore his passion for martial arts and expand his creative abilities behind the camera.

Chapter 4

The Matrix Trilogy

"The Matrix" trilogy consists of three science fiction films: "The Matrix" (1999), "The Matrix Reloaded" (2003), and "The Matrix Revolutions" (2003). Keanu Reeves played the lead role of Neo, a computer programmer who discovers that the world he knows is actually a simulated reality created by sentient machines.

In the first film, "The Matrix," Neo is recruited by a group of rebels led by Morpheus, played by Laurence Fishburne, to fight against the machines and free humanity from their control. Reeves' portrayal of Neo was praised for his ability to balance the character's vulnerability and determination, making him a relatable and compelling protagonist.

In the sequels, "The Matrix Reloaded" and "The Matrix Revolutions," Neo continues his journey to understand the true nature of the Matrix and his role in the war against the machines. Reeves' performance in these films showcased his physicality and agility, as he engaged in intense action sequences and martial arts battles.

The "Matrix" trilogy was groundbreaking in its visual effects and philosophical themes, exploring concepts of reality, identity, and the nature of existence. Keanu Reeves' portrayal of Neo became iconic, and the trilogy as a whole has had a lasting impact on popular culture.

"The Matrix" trilogy, directed by the Wachowskis, revolutionized the science fiction genre with its groundbreaking visual effects, complex storytelling, and philosophical themes. Keanu Reeves' portrayal of Neo, the chosen one who fights against the machines, played a crucial role in the success and popularity of the trilogy.

In "The Matrix," Neo is introduced as a disillusioned computer programmer who is searching for answers about the nature of reality. When he encounters the enigmatic Morpheus, played by Laurence Fishburne, Neo is offered the choice to take a red pill and awaken to the truth or continue living in the simulated reality known as the Matrix.

Reeves' performance as Neo was praised for his ability to bring a sense of vulnerability and determination to the character. He seamlessly transitioned from a curious and skeptical individual to a skilled fighter and leader. Reeves' physicality and dedication to the role were evident in the intense action sequences, where he performed many of his own stunts.

In the sequels, "The Matrix Reloaded" and "The Matrix Revolutions," Neo's journey continues as he delves deeper into the mysteries of the Matrix and confronts the machines in the real world. Reeves' portrayal of Neo evolved, showcasing his growth as a character and his willingness to sacrifice for the greater good.

The "Matrix" trilogy not only showcased Reeves' skills as an action star but also allowed him to explore deeper philosophical themes. The trilogy raised questions about the nature of reality, free will, and the power of choice, making it more than just a typical action franchise.

Keanu Reeves' involvement in "The Matrix" trilogy solidified his status as a Hollywood leading man and further established his reputation as a versatile actor. His dedication to the role and his ability to bring depth and complexity to Neo made him an integral part of the trilogy's success.

Chapter 5

Action Star Status

Keanu Reeves is a renowned action star in the film industry. With his impressive acting skills and captivating screen presence, he has established himself as one of the most beloved and iconic action heroes of our time. From his breakout role as Neo in "The Matrix" trilogy to his intense performances in films like "John Wick" and "Speed," Reeves has consistently delivered thrilling and memorable action sequences. His dedication to performing his own stunts and his commitment to bringing authenticity to his characters have further solidified his status as an action star. Keanu Reeves continues to captivate audiences worldwide with his unparalleled charisma and remarkable talent in the action genre.

In addition to his action-packed filmography, Keanu Reeves has also become known for his humble and down-to-earth personality off-screen. Despite his immense success, he remains grounded and approachable, often taking the time to interact with fans and show gratitude for their support. This genuine connection with his audience has only further endeared him to fans around the world.

Reeves' dedication to his craft goes beyond just his physical performances. He is known for immersing himself in the roles he takes on, often undergoing extensive training to fully embody his characters. Whether it's learning martial arts for "The Matrix" or mastering tactical gunplay for "John Wick," he consistently pushes himself to deliver the most authentic and believable performances possible.

Beyond his action star status, Keanu Reeves has also showcased his versatility as an actor in a variety of other genres. From his heartfelt performance in "The Devil's Advocate" to his comedic timing in "Bill & Ted's Excellent Adventure," he has proven time and time again that he can excel in any role he takes on.

With his undeniable talent, genuine personality, and unwavering commitment to his craft, Keanu Reeves has undoubtedly earned his place as one of the most respected and beloved action stars in the industry. His impact on the genre and his ability to connect with audiences make him a true icon in the world of action cinema.

Chapter 6

Philanthropy and Personal Life

Philosophy:
Keanu Reeves has often expressed his philosophical views in various interviews and public appearances. One of his notable beliefs is the importance of empathy and compassion. He has spoken about the need for kindness and understanding in the world, emphasizing the significance of connecting with others on a deeper level.

Reeves also embraces a humble and down-to-earth attitude, despite his fame and success. He often emphasizes the importance of staying true to oneself and remaining grounded, even in the face of stardom. This philosophy has resonated with many fans and has contributed to Reeves' reputation as a genuine and relatable celebrity.

Keanu Reeves has often spoken about the transformative power of art and storytelling. He believes that movies and other forms of artistic expression have the ability to inspire, provoke thought, and create meaningful connections between people. Reeves has expressed his love for the creative process and the impact that stories can have on individuals and society as a whole.

Reeves also values the importance of personal growth and self-improvement. He has spoken about the need to continually learn, evolve, and challenge oneself. This mindset has led him to take on a variety of roles in different genres, pushing his boundaries as an actor and exploring new artistic territories.

Personal Life:
Keanu Reeves has had his fair share of personal challenges throughout his life. He has experienced tragic losses, including the deaths of his girlfriend, Jennifer Syme, and their unborn child. These events have had a profound impact on him, leading him to reflect on the

fragility of life and the importance of cherishing every moment.

Despite these hardships, Reeves has shown resilience and a positive outlook. He is known for his generosity, often donating a significant portion of his earnings to charitable causes. Additionally, he has been involved in several philanthropic endeavors, including supporting cancer research and children's hospitals.

Reeves is also an avid motorcyclist and has a passion for riding. He has been spotted riding motorcycles both on and off-screen, and he even co-founded a motorcycle manufacturing company called Arch Motorcycle Company.

In addition to his acting career, Keanu Reeves has pursued other creative endeavors. He is a talented musician and has played bass guitar in the alternative rock band Dogstar in the 1990s. Reeves has also dabbled in directing, with his directorial debut "Man of Tai Chi" released in 2013.

Despite his fame, Reeves is known for leading a relatively private and low-key personal life. He maintains a down-to-earth approach and often avoids the spotlight when he is not working. This has contributed to his reputation as a humble and grounded individual.

Reeves is an avid reader and has a deep interest in literature and philosophy. He has mentioned authors such as Fyodor Dostoevsky, Hermann Hesse, and Jack Kerouac as influences on his thinking and artistic sensibilities.

In recent years, Reeves has experienced a career resurgence and has been praised for his performances in films like "John Wick" and "The Matrix" series. He continues to be highly regarded by both critics and audiences, and his popularity shows no signs of waning.

Chapter 7

Career Resurgence

Keanu Reeves' career resurgence has been a notable highlight in recent years. After a period of relatively quieter roles, he experienced a major comeback with his portrayal of John Wick in the eponymous action film series.

Released in 2014, "John Wick" became a surprise hit and garnered critical acclaim for its intense action sequences and Reeves' compelling performance. The film's success led to two highly successful sequels, "John Wick: Chapter 2" (2017) and "John Wick: Chapter 3 – Parabellum" (2019), further solidifying Reeves' status as an action star.

In addition to the "John Wick" series, Reeves also returned to another iconic role in "The Matrix" franchise. The fourth installment, "The Matrix Resurrections," is set to be released in 2021, bringing back Reeves as Neo, the iconic character he portrayed in the original trilogy.

Reeves' career resurgence has been marked by a renewed appreciation from both critics and audiences. His performances in these action-packed films have showcased his physicality, intensity, and dedication to his craft. Fans have praised his ability to bring depth and emotional resonance to his characters, even in the midst of adrenaline-fueled action sequences.

Beyond his action roles, Reeves has also taken on diverse projects, showcasing his versatility as an actor. He starred in the romantic drama "Always Be My Maybe" (2019), where he played a hilarious and self-parodying version of himself. This role further endeared him to audiences and demonstrated his ability to embrace different genres and styles.

In addition to his successful action films, Keanu Reeves has also ventured into other genres and showcased his range as an actor. He starred in the romantic drama "The Lake House" (2006) alongside Sandra Bullock, which received positive reviews for their on-screen chemistry and heartfelt performances.

Reeves also took on the role of a police officer in the crime thriller "Street Kings" (2008), directed by David Ayer. The film received mixed reviews but allowed Reeves to explore a darker and grittier character.

In recent years, Reeves has also embraced the world of voice acting. He lent his voice to the character Duke Caboom in the animated film "Toy Story 4" (2019), which was well-received by both critics and audiences.

Reeves' career resurgence has not been limited to the big screen. He has also made a successful transition to the television medium. In 2019, he starred in the Netflix film "Always Be My Maybe" and made a memorable cameo appearance as a heightened version of himself. The scene garnered widespread attention and praise for his comedic timing and willingness to poke fun at his own persona.

Furthermore, Reeves has been cast in highly anticipated projects, including "The Batman" (2022), where he will portray the iconic character of Batman's ally, Commissioner Gordon. This casting choice has generated excitement among fans, further solidifying Reeves' position as a sought-after actor in the industry.

Overall, Keanu Reeves' career resurgence has been marked by a diverse range of roles and a willingness to explore different genres and mediums. His ability to captivate audiences with his performances, whether in action films, dramas, or comedies, has cemented his status as a versatile and beloved actor in Hollywood.

Chapter 8

John Wick Franchise

The John Wick franchise has become one of Keanu Reeves' most iconic and successful film series. The franchise follows the story of a retired hitman named John Wick, who seeks revenge after the theft of his beloved car and the killing of his dog, which was a final gift from his deceased wife.

The first film, simply titled "John Wick," was released in 2014 and was directed by Chad Stahelski, a former stuntman and Reeves' longtime collaborator. The movie was praised for its stylish action sequences, intense fight choreography, and Reeves' committed performance. It quickly gained a cult following and became a surprise hit at the box office.

The success of the first film led to the release of two highly anticipated sequels. "John Wick: Chapter 2" was released in 2017 and further expanded the world and mythology of the franchise. The film delved deeper into the criminal underworld and introduced new characters and alliances. It was praised for its inventive action sequences and continued to showcase Reeves' physicality and dedication to the role.

The third installment, "John Wick: Chapter 3 – Parabellum," was released in 2019 and continued the story immediately after the events of the second film. This installment saw John Wick on the run from a global network of assassins, and it further explored the intricacies of the assassin world. Like its predecessors, the film was lauded for its high-octane action and Reeves' committed performance.

The John Wick franchise has been praised for its unique blend of stylish action, intricate world-building, and compelling characters. It has garnered a dedicated fan base and has solidified Keanu Reeves' status as an action star. The franchise's success has also led to the development of a spin-off television series titled "The Continental," which will focus on the hotel for assassins featured in the films.

Overall, the John Wick franchise has become a significant part of Keanu Reeves' career, showcasing his talents as an action star and his ability to bring depth and humanity to his characters. The series has cemented his status as one of the most beloved and respected actors in the action genre.

Chapter 9

Other Notable Films

Keanu Reeves is known for his diverse filmography and has appeared in numerous notable films throughout his career. In addition to his iconic role as Neo in "The Matrix" trilogy, some of his other notable films include:

1. "Speed" (1994) - In this action thriller, Reeves plays a police officer who must prevent a bomb from exploding on a city bus.

2. "John Wick" series (2014-present) - Reeves portrays the titular character, a legendary assassin seeking vengeance for the death of his dog.
3. "Point Break" (1991) - He stars as an undercover FBI agent who infiltrates a group of bank-robbing surfers.
4. "Bill & Ted's Excellent Adventure" (1989) and "Bill & Ted's Bogus Journey" (1991) - Reeves plays Ted Theodore Logan, one-half of the time-traveling duo in these cult comedy films.
5. "The Devil's Advocate" (1997) - Reeves portrays a defense attorney who becomes embroiled in a sinister world

after joining a prestigious law firm.
6. "Constantine" (2005) - He takes on the role of John Constantine, a supernatural detective battling demons and other dark forces.
7. "The Replacements" (2000) - Reeves plays a former football player who is recruited to lead a team of replacement players during a professional football strike.
8. "A Scanner Darkly" (2006) - In this animated sci-fi film, Reeves stars as an undercover cop in a dystopian future.
9. "Speed 2: Cruise Control" (1997) - Reeves did not reprise his role from the first "Speed" film, but it's worth mentioning

the sequel, in which he was replaced by Jason Patric.
10. "The Lake House" (2006) - Reeves stars opposite Sandra Bullock in this romantic drama about two people who communicate across time through a magical mailbox.
11. "Hardball" (2001) - Reeves portrays a gambler who coaches a youth baseball team in a disadvantaged neighborhood.
12. "The Devil's Advocate" (1997) - Reeves plays a talented lawyer who finds himself in a Faustian bargain when he joins a powerful law firm.
13. "My Own Private Idaho" (1991) - He shares the screen with River Phoenix in this independent drama about two

young hustlers navigating life on the streets of Portland.

14. "Man of Tai Chi" (2013) - Reeves makes his directorial debut and plays the villain in this martial arts film about a talented fighter who becomes entangled in the dangerous world of underground fighting.
15. "The Day the Earth Stood Still" (2008) - Reeves stars as an alien who arrives on Earth to deliver a warning to humanity.
16. "Knock Knock" (2015) - In this thriller, Reeves plays a family man who becomes the target of two seductive and manipulative women.
17. "47 Ronin" (2013) - Reeves leads a group of samurai warriors seeking revenge in

this fantasy action film inspired by Japanese folklore.
18. "Replicas" (2018) - Reeves plays a scientist who clones his family members after a tragic accident.
20. "Parenthood" (1989) - Reeves has a supporting role in this comedy-drama about the joys and challenges of parenting.
21. "The Gift" (2000) - He portrays a violent and abusive husband in this psychological thriller directed by Sam Raimi.
22. "Something's Gotta Give" (2003) - Reeves appears in a supporting role as a young doctor in this romantic comedy starring Jack Nicholson and Diane Keaton.
23. "Street Kings" (2008) - Reeves plays a troubled LAPD

detective caught up in a web of corruption in this crime thriller.

24. "The Neon Demon" (2016) - Reeves has a small role as a sleazy motel manager in this psychological horror film directed by Nicolas Winding Refn.
25. "The Bad Batch" (2016) - He portrays a charismatic cult leader in this dystopian thriller set in a post-apocalyptic Texas.
26. "To the Bone" (2017) - Reeves has a supporting role as a doctor in this drama about a young woman struggling with anorexia.
27. "Siberia" (2018) - He stars as a diamond merchant embroiled in a dangerous

underworld deal in this crime thriller.
28. "Always Be My Maybe" (2019) - Reeves makes a hilarious cameo appearance as a fictionalized version of himself in this romantic comedy.
29. "Destination Wedding" (2018) - Reeves reunites with Winona Ryder in this romantic comedy about two strangers who develop a connection while attending a destination wedding.
30. "The Matrix Resurrections" (2021) - While not released at the time of my knowledge cutoff, Keanu Reeves is set to reprise his iconic role as Neo in the highly anticipated fourth installment of "The Matrix" franchise.

31. River's Edge" (1986) - Reeves stars as a teenager who discovers that his friend has murdered his girlfriend in this dark drama.
32. "Feeling Minnesota" (1996) - He plays a drifter who becomes entangled in a love triangle in this crime comedy-drama.
33. "The Last Time I Committed Suicide" (1997) - Reeves portrays the American beat poet Neal Cassady in this biographical drama.
34. "The Watcher" (2000) - He plays an FBI agent pursuing a serial killer in this psychological thriller.
35. "Sweet November" (2001) - Reeves stars opposite Charlize Theron in this romantic drama

about a man who falls in love with a woman who has a terminal illness.
36. "Street Kings" (2008) - He portrays a detective who becomes implicated in a conspiracy in this crime thriller.
37. "Generation Um..." (2012) - Reeves plays a man who spends a day with two young women, examining their lives and exploring their personal struggles.
38. "Exposed" (2016) - He plays a detective investigating the death of his partner while encountering supernatural forces in this crime thriller.
39. "The Whole Truth" (2016) - Reeves portrays a defense attorney representing a

Keanu Reeves

teenager accused of murdering his wealthy father in this courtroom drama.

Chapter 10

Awards and Recognition

Keanu Reeves has received several awards and recognition throughout his career. While he may not have won many major awards, his contributions to the film industry have been acknowledged by various organizations and his performances have garnered critical acclaim. Here are some of the notable awards and recognition received by Keanu Reeves:

1. MTV Movie Awards:
     - Best Male Performance for "The Matrix" (2000)
     - Best Fight for "The Matrix" (shared with Laurence Fishburne) (2000)
     - Best On-Screen Duo for "The Matrix" (shared with Laurence Fishburne) (2000)
     - Best Hero for "The Matrix Reloaded" (2004)
     - Best Fight for "John Wick" (shared with Adrianne Palicki) (2015)
     - Best Action Performance for "John Wick: Chapter 2" (2018)
2. Hollywood Walk of Fame:
     - Star on the Hollywood Walk of Fame (2005)

3. Saturn Awards:
   - Best Actor for "Speed" (1995)
   - Best Actor for "The Matrix" (2000)
   - Best Actor for "John Wick" (2015)
4. Blockbuster Entertainment Awards:
   - Favorite Actor - Action/Adventure for "The Matrix" (2000)
5. Hollywood Film Festival:
   - Actor of the Year Award (2006)
6. Canadian Screen Awards:
   - Golden Screen Award for Highest Grossing Canadian Film for "John Wick" (2016)
7. National Movie Awards (UK):

- Best Performance - Male for "John Wick: Chapter 2" (2017)
8. Hollywood Critics Association:
    - The Action Icon Award (2019)
9. Taurus World Stunt Awards:
    - Best Fight for "John Wick" (shared with Daniel Bernhardt) (2015)
10. Critics' Choice Movie Awards:
    - Best Actor in an Action Movie for "John Wick" (2015)
11. Canadian Academy of Cinema and Television:
    - Canadian Screen Awards - Fan Choice Award (2020)
12. Golden Schmoes Awards:
    - Best Actor of the Year for "John Wick" (2014)

13. Hollywood Film Awards:
    - Hollywood Career Achievement Award (2019)
14. Teen Choice Awards:
    - Choice Movie Actor: Drama for "The Lake House" (2006)
    - Choice Movie Actor: Action for "John Wick: Chapter 2" (2017)
    - Choice Movie: Liplock for "John Wick: Chapter 2" (shared with Ruby Rose) (2017)
15. Spike Video Game Awards:
    - Best Performance by a Human Male for voicing the character of John Wick in "John Wick Hex" (2020)

These additional awards and recognition highlight Keanu Reeves' impact and appeal in the film industry. Despite not receiving numerous major awards, his performances and contributions have been acknowledged by various organizations and his work continues to resonate with audiences.

Conclusion

As we come to the end of "Keanu Reeves: The Life and Career of Keanu Reeves," it is evident that the story of this enigmatic actor is as captivating as the characters he portrays on the silver screen. From his humble beginnings to his rise to international stardom, Keanu Reeves' journey is a testament to resilience, dedication, and a genuine passion for the craft of acting.

Throughout the pages of this biography, we have delved into the behind-the-scenes moments that shaped his iconic roles, the challenges he faced in his personal life, and the profound impact he has had on both the film industry and popular culture. From Neo in "The Matrix" to John Wick in the adrenaline-pumping action films,

Reeves' versatility as an actor has left an indelible mark on cinema.

Beyond the fame and fortune, Keanu Reeves has shown a remarkable depth of character. His philanthropic efforts and acts of kindness have endeared him to fans worldwide, making him more than just an actor but a true role model for many.

As we bid farewell to the pages of this book, it becomes clear that Keanu Reeves' journey is far from over. With new projects on the horizon and a legacy that continues to inspire, his impact will undoubtedly endure for generations to come.

To all the readers who have embarked on this journey, thank you for joining us in celebrating the life and career of Keanu Reeves. May his story continue to ignite the imagination and inspire us to face life's challenges with grace and resilience, just as he has done throughout his extraordinary career.

As Keanu Reeves continues to grace the silver screen with his presence, let us remember that his story is not just about the characters he plays, but the real-life hero who has captured our hearts and left an everlasting impression on the world of cinema.

In the spirit of Keanu Reeves, let us embrace kindness,

compassion, and a love for the art that unites us all. As we close this chapter, may we carry the lessons learned from his journey and continue to be inspired by the indomitable spirit of this remarkable actor.

Thank you for being a part of this remarkable adventure, and here's to the enduring legacy of Keanu Reeves – a true cinematic legend.

Printed in Great Britain
by Amazon